Shapes: Squares

Esther Sarfatti

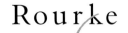

Rourke
Publishing LLC
Vero Beach, Florida 32964

www.rourkepublishing.com

PHOTO CREDITS: © Jim Lopes: page 5; © Radu Razvan: page 7; © Sean Locke and Nicholas Belton: page 9; © Andrew Johnson: page 11; © M. Eric Honeycutt: page 13; © Don Joski: page 15; © Vorakorn Tuvajitt: page 17; © Rebecca Paul: page 19; © Tomasz Tulik: page 21; © Flavia Bottazzini: page 23.

Editor: Robert Stengard-Olliges

Cover design by Nicola Stratford.

Library of Congress Cataloging-in-Publication Data

Sarfatti, Esther.
  Shapes : squares / Esther Sarfatti.
     p. cm. -- (Concepts)
  ISBN 978-1-60044-527-9 (Hardcover)
  ISBN 978-1-60044-668-9 (Softcover)
 1. Rectangles--Juvenile literature. 2. Shapes--Juvenile literature. I. Title.
  QA484.S269 2008
  516'.154--dc22
                            2007014075

Printed in the USA

CG/CG

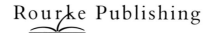

Rourke Publishing

www.rourkepublishing.com – rourke@rourkepublishing.com
Post Office Box 3328, Vero Beach, FL 32964

This is a square.

Squares are everywhere.

These crackers are square.

This picture is square.

This puzzle is square.

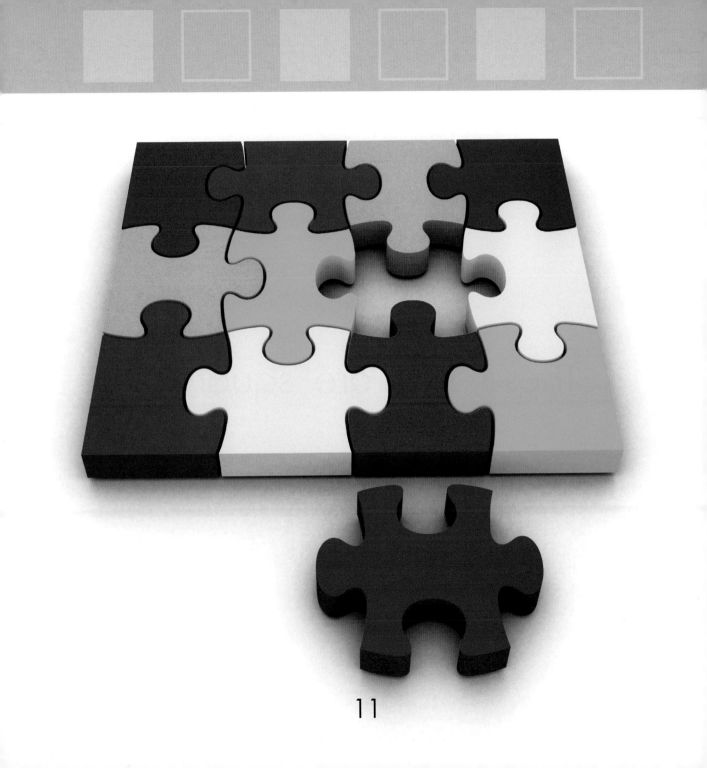

These tiles are squares.

These pillows are squares.

These brownies are squares.

This clock is a square.

19

These ice cubes are squares.

21

Squares are everywhere.
Can you find the squares?

23

Index

brownies   16
crackers   6
pillows   14
puzzle   10

Further Reading

Leake, Diyan. *Finding Shapes: Squares*. Heinemann, 2005.
Olson, Nathan. *Squares Around Town*. A+ Books, 2007.

Recommended Websites

www.enchantedlearning.com/themes/shapes.shtml

About the Author

Esther Sarfatti has worked with children's books for over 15 years as an editor and translator. This is her first series as an author. Born in Brooklyn, New York, and brought up in a trilingual home, Esther currently lives with her husband and son in Madrid, Spain.